To journal is the path to self discovery through the depths of your inner deepest thoughts without fear nor boundaries.

-Yasmin Isabel Velasquez.

DEAR DIARY.......

Do you ever feel like nobody in this world cares about you or loves you?
I feel like I have no real connection to anybody not even my friends, family, significant others I have had, co-workers, etc. Maybe, I don't even have a connection to myself. I am constantly in denial of my own truths. I find that I self sabotage my own life and I am aware the whole time but someway somehow, I find a way to be surprised at myself or at the outcome every single time. I do not know why I do this to myself...... I can't help but ask myself whenever I sit alone with my thoughts....do I enjoy pain? Do I inflict pain into my life subconsciously to be a victim to prevent myself from seeing my own flaws and facing my very own problems?

DEAR DIARY.......

Growing up, I was always known as the girl that would always laugh and smile all the time. Everyone I've gone to school with always thought my life was great and loved my positive energy. However, they had no idea the hell I would go through mentally and at home. School was a place where I can temporaily escape my problems and suicidal thoughts I had at the time. I bet no one knew I was suicidal for twelve years and have attempted two times in my life. I thought about death every single day and how I can just rid myself of the agony of everyday life if I just died. Truth was, later down the line, I found out that I didn't want to die, I just wanted to be saved. I saved myself because if I wasn't, who was going to? Everything will be clearer later.

DEAR DIARY.......

Anyways, let me provide an example of me self sabotaging my life, so not too long ago I dated this guy that I absolutely did not trust and never have. To my ever "shocking" surprise, he was leading me on, lying to me, and looking for the love of his life at the same time while he was with me and while he was telling me I was the only girl he wanted to be with or liked....the whole time. Upon finding out the news, my heart was shattered and I said harsh things about myself. I said I wasn't good enough for him, I'm not attractive enough, why would he pick her over me, I wasn't interesting enough, I didn't understand him enough, etc. I felt like utter and complete shit about myself. I was crying and sitting in my own self pity for hours.

DEAR DIARY.......

I acted like a whole victim, yet I knew we were not going to last. He use to text me back hours, days, and sometimes weeks later due to his "overwhelming" and "busy" life. We hardly EVER met up because either his job was too far, he was too busy, or has to do something once he got home. Mind you, we live in the same state. I always asked to meet half way but still meeting up was impossible. He eventually got a job super near where I live and STILL couldn't make the time to meet up with me. Those were major red flags and I ignored them because I loved him and wanted to hope that things would've worked out. People make time for the things they want to do and the people they want to see. The truth was, he just didn't want to see me.

DEAR DIARY.......

I ignored that truth about him because I thought maybe if I tried to believe him, that truth wouldn't be.....true. That truth was painful to think about. I could not wrap my head around, why a guy I did so much for.....NOT want to see me? I wanted to be his everything, his girlfriend, his therapist, his chef, his muse, his calm after the storm, something he looked forward to everyday, etc. I went on all day wondering why I wasn't good enough or worthy of him asking me officially to be his girlfriend or let alone put effort to show me he even gave a damn about me. I asked myself, what did she do that I didn't do? Did she understand him better, is she prettier than me, did she do more for him than I did (even though I know she didn't), etc. So many questions.

DEAR DIARY.......

I knew he wasn't shit the moment I knew him and the moment he tried to pursue me but I still....gave him the benefit of the doubt and went along with it....in hopes that I wouldn't get my heart broken. I believe that at one point, I actually believed it too because I have done so much for this guy that hasn't done that much for me. I have brought him food, surprises at work when he wasn't feeling well, words of encouragement, made his problems my problems, made his birthdays special, sent a sweet long "Happy Birthday" message at midnight, sent money to cheer him up a bit even if it was just enough to buy lunch, tried to plan out fun activities to do to lift his spirits or just have fun since he was always working all the time, etc.

DEAR DIARY......

In return, I was ghosted a lot without explanation or would get an explanation after continuous effort to get an explanation, excuses to not meet up with me, get frustrated when I would say he doesn't text or see me often, nothing for my birthday, nothing for Valentine's Day, never took me out on a date like he said he would because he was "serious" about it, would causally say I can have sex with other people (yuck), etc. Him saying I can have sex with other people always rubbed me the wrong way and made me feel as though he was doing that himself but would feel better about it if I was doing it too. Lord and behold, he was dating someone else at the same time while deceiving and leading me on the whole time.

DEAR DIARY.......

No wonder why we would never meet up in public places only his car or private places. He wanted to cover his tracks. The signs were all there yet when all was said to me, I acted as if I was surprised and woo is me but deep down, I knew we were not going to last.... I just wanted to enjoy the time I had left with him however long that was because maybe just maybe a part of me had hoped things would've turned out differently than I had expected and that would've been the person I spend the rest of my life with to be happy and rid myself of the constant existential loneliness that I feel everyday especially whenever I am alone, see happy couples, or whenever I am surrounded by a lot of joyful people talking and having a blast doing so.

DEAR DIARY.......

I honestly should've known better and everyone else was right about him. Even my intuition knew he wasn't shit. Lesson learned though. Always follow your intuition, if something feels off then it probably is, listen to other people sometimes since they are not in love with them so they are not a bias opinion, etc. I shoulv'e known by the way he treats others too. He says he does this to everyone not just me so I shouldn't take it personal but that doesn't mean all the people in his life have to deal with that. Moral of the story is, he used me to get what he wanted, to not feel lonely, feed his ego, etc. He preys on vulnerable women. Everytime he has tried to pursue me.... it has always been in a very vulnerable state.

DEAR DIARY.......

Yes I have dated him twice. The first time was a couple years ago, I ended things shortly because he was texting me once every five days and I was fed up. Second and last time was recent and lasted for almost a year. He is the same exact person, just better at manipulating women and acting like a victim at first to come across as a caring loving man who keeps getting hurt by women while in reality, he is full of shit and the one hurting women instead. The first time we dated was shortly after my boyfriend at the time cheated on me and I came to him for emotional support since he was a good friend to me. He tried to date me shortly after and I agreed to do so after I had some time to heal and he changed the way he acted towards me.

DEAR DIARY……

He was super consistent with me and checking up with me but then once he got me, he turned super sexual, kept trying to manipulate me into doing things I did not want to do, and was an asshole to be honest. Fast forward a few years later (about six), he came to me when I was in a vulnerable state again after my boyfriend at the time (different guy from the one that cheated on me) physically abused me. It was a year and five months of me being in a very emotionally abusive and unloving relationship. I was always doing everything, he was not emotionally available whatsoever, rude to my friends, shallow, super unromantic, judgmental, emotionless, never really met up with me always wanted me to come to him, etc.

DEAR DIARY.......

I was in a super emotional state after that abusive encounter with my ex and he was there for me after not speaking to me for almost six years. I was healing, he checked up on me, invited me out with his bestfriend, drove me home, was a consistent texter, sweet, caring, and mentioned hanging out often. After about two or three months or so, I decided to date him since he wanted to earlier but I was not emotionally ready to go back into dating. It seemed as though he had changed but you guys already know that wasn't the case. It was the same shit once he got me again. Going back to an ex or a person you use to date..... you got to be careful because most likely it will end again for similar reasons unfortunately.

DEAR DIARY.......

I find myself in these constant cycles of dating someone I know I will not be with long term and I am not entirely sure why. Is it because I don't want to be alone, feel alone, do I even actually like them or the idea of them, am I obsessed with them changing their toxic ways because of me, am I attracted to broken men, have something to look forward to everyday since I hardly have any friends, etc. To be honest, it is probably all of the above because a lot of these men I've dated aren't even all that. My abusive ex for example was not even that attractive, boring to talk to more than half of the time, selfish, narcissistic, a gaslighter, lazy, rude, etc yet I was so attached and drawn to him like a moth to a flame.

DEAR DIARY.......

I think I was drawn to the attention he would give me every single day. It is really nice to have a person to talk to every single day throughout the day. It makes me feel like someone out there is thinking of me, wants to talk to me, make me a part of their day, makes me feel less lonely, makes me less likely to sit in my room at night and ponder about my loneliness, think about how I have nobody that loves me, and makes me have something to look forward to everyday even if it is just a text message. It makes me feel as though I am not bothering anyone because when dating, constant communication is expected while with friends, sometimes constant communication can be an annoyance or make me feel like I am bothering them.

DEAR DIARY.......

One thing I always hated as a child growing up was feeling like a burden or like I am bothering someone. My parents (I don't think they were fully aware) would always indirectly say how life was basically better before I was born. They would talk about how life was easier, how they didn't have any health problems, how happy they were, and how life would have been better if they didn't have any kids. My parents are toxic together and I know they only stay in each other's lives because of me. That makes me feel like it is my fault they are suffering now. I feel like a burden at times like maybe life would have been better for them and everyone if I was never born or just disappeared one day. I really wonder how their lives would've been without me.

DEAR DIARY.......

They say they love me all the time but sometimes I wonder how much. I mean I barely have a real connection with them, have little to nothing to talk about, don't really spend quality time together, etc. On the other hand, maybe they do because there are times they are super clingy, ask me if I love them, tell me they love me, and do try to spend time with me. On the other hand, at times I can be a bit confused at how much they actually care or love me because of their toxic behavior towards me at times. Every year on my birthday, they tell me nobody loves me except them and ask who texted me "Happy Birthday" and I lie and say nobody because I grew up sheltered and it has always been an issue if I had friends so I pretend I don't have any.

DEAR DIARY.......

I like to avoid drama in my life so to my parent's knowledge (especially my dad), I do NOT have friends and never ever will lol. Back when my dad knew about my friends, he would stalk us from afar to see what we were doing while hanging out. It made me uncomfortable. He would also check my phone call/text records every month to see which numbers I am interacting with. If he saw that I was interacting with a number too often, he would ask me about it and I hated that. It made me not wanna call or text anybody. One time, he found out I had a boyfriend and made my life a living hell. He stalked me at college, would get furious with me if I left class a few minutes late, would send me threats via text message, and would just be plain cruel to me.

DEAR DIARY.......

My dad is just a very toxic awful human being with some good in him. He can be generous at times and spoil me but the negatives surpass the positives. I mean he can't properly love someone, he has cheated on his wife (not my mom) everyday for decades, has three baby mommas, selfish, narcissistic, a pathological liar, gaslights all the time, bad temper, yells too much at anyone that disagrees with him, racist, pervert, and has messed up ideologies about women such as believing they should get raped if they're wearing a provocative outfit because they "asked" for it, etc. He has little to no morals I mean this is the very same man that makes it obvious he is in love with my aunt but lies about it all the time to cover his tracks.

DEAR DIARY.......

My dad will project his frustrations onto me when I have nothing to do with his problems. I can never disagree with him because he will start yelling and say harsh disrespectful things to me. For example, one time I was telling him he should stop eating fried fish since he has high cholesterol and he got so mad at me and was saying it is not bad for his health and said that my head was full of shit. Uncalled for completely. I am use to this verbal abuse growing up. My mom will make a mistake and blame it on me. They have trouble taking accountability or being responsible of their actions. For example, she will drop something on the ground and then get mad at tell me "look what you made me do" even if I was nowhere near.

DEAR DIARY.......

It goes far deeper but the verbal abuse and manipulation of making me believe no one loves me has manifested itself into me believing it. Patterns I have noticed and past relationships have led me to believe these things. With friendships, I feel like none of them actually care that much about me. They will either be jealous of me, act shady, make me a back up plan if someone else cancels plans with them, expect me to be there for them but with me they are half ass there or not at all, use me, habitually lie to me, etc. I have people I consider friends but in reality there is no one I feel like I can truly open up to and know that they will be there for me and actucally love me as a friend for who I am rather than the benefits of being my friend.

DEAR DIARY.......

I believe I am a good friend. I will always be there for you, be a listening ear, have your back, surprise you, make you feel good about yourself, won't judge you, be kind to you, and most of all be very honest. Friends I make know this and use this to their advantage I feel. The same energy and love is never reciprocated. I said earlier that they are jealous of me and I feel that way because it seems like they can never be happy for me and my achievements. They always just seem so neutral and never have much to say whenever I have good news but have a lot more to say when I have bad news. As mean as this sounds, I feel like they are jealous because they do not have much going on in their lives, no goals, no job, settling for medicore relationships, etc.

DEAR DIARY.......

I have never been in any competition with my friends but I can tell they see I have goals, ambitions, I'm going somewhere, emotionally strong, intelligent, I have a job, people tend to be drawn to me, etc. They even have mentioned how I am the one doing better than everyone else in the friend group and have the most money. I do not do it on purpose, I just want the best life for myself that I can possibility obtain. I always felt like they think I just show off but that's not the case. I even have tried to help them by giving them advice on how to make money, how to own a business, how to love themselves more, how to be more motivated in life, etc. I have always been their therapist but when my soul is weeping, they're nowhere to be found.

DEAR DIARY.......

I even had this one friend that always told me that she loves me but would always do some weird ass shit. Every guy I was dating, she would always try to sit on their lap, kiss their cheek, touch them a lot, tried to have sex with one of them, text them a lot, etc. When me and whoever I was dating were in bad terms, she wouldn't be there for me and would spend a lot of time with them like EXTRA time and even sit on their lap longer. She always did it in front of me. There were times she would be passive aggressive towards me too for no reason. I think she would project her insecurities towards me a lot. Truth was, that girl was just fake and I should've ended my friendship with her a long time ago and my relationship with the guy(s) for allowng it.

DEAR DIARY.......

I find myself overextending myself for all the people I care about in life but who overextends for me? Who wonders how I am feeling? Who actually thinks about me? For my family and friends, I have bought them foods they said they have been craving, random things they said they wanted, and would try to make them feel special for their birthdays. I never had someone like that in life..... someone who wants to put in effort to make me feel special, happy, and or loved. I will admit with boyfriends, I always found myself treating them way better than anyone else in my life. Now for my boyfriends I have crossed roads, climbed mountains, and walked through the coldest of snow storms to make them feel loved and cared about.

DEAR DIARY.......

Whenever I am with someone, I do so much more for them than I even do for myself. I try to build them, solve their problems, buy them things they want and need, buy them flowers, cook for them, constantly try to surprise them with gifts, shower them with affection, check up on them when they're depressed, always planning something thoughtful to do for them, get them something for their birthday, text them a long sweet paragraph on their birthday exactly at midnight, plan out a day of romance for them on Valentine's Day, and the list goes on and on. I never had a guy care about me like that, reciprocate similar energy, or do anything for me coming from a place of genuine love. I never have even gotten flowers before.

DEAR DIARY……

Instead, I get these manipulative, lying, deceiving, emotionally unavailable, selfish, occasionally caring, gaslighting, cheating, bullying, and abusive men. Whenever the break up is all said and done, they ALWAYS appear fine, don't fight to keep the relationship, move on fast, never contact me again, and just seem happier. It really makes me feel like….. am I really that disposable and replaceable? When the break up is all said and done, I am a whole mess. I am crying, questioning my self worth, can barely eat, cry myself to sleep, listen to music to calm myself, cry alone in my room at night, get sad randomly when I see something that reminds me of them or the good times we have had, etc. We just go back to being strangers after everything.

DEAR DIARY.......

I am all chocked up when I see that they are doing just fine without me while I am falling to pieces and falling apart knowing how I treated them and how bad they treated me. After so much refection back on my life, I think I do so much for my partner because I want to try everything I can to keep them interested, keep the relationship, and just have something to look forward to everyday. I love love and to feel loved. Love is something I have lacked my entire life. You already know what I said about my current friends previously, but before the friends I have now, I grew up making friends that pretended to be my friend out of pity and was incredibly embarrassed of being my friend because I was very obese growing up.

DEAR DIARY.......

I never felt attractive until I started to lose weight and it wasn't until I lost weight that people actually wanted to be my friend or be with me romantically. People can be so shallow sometimes. It made me wonder if my personality alone was enough to make people want to be in my life and stay. Men I have dated in my past life did not help either. One guy I dated on and off for four years use to always tell me I would look so much better if I lose weight and get a much bigger ass. He use to compare me to "IG models" saying that any guy would get distracted or want more from me body wise after seeing how "crazy good" their bodies look. It made me feel self conscious because it made me feel as though I was not attractive.

DEAR DIARY.......

He use to always call me pretty but it never felt enough since he would always want more from me as far as body appearance goes. I was already struggling with my self image growing up due to being obese and I was learning to appreciate and love my body after losing that weight. He never embraced what I had, only made me feel bad about what I have yet I stayed a very long time tolerating his verbally abusive behavior because I was attached to him. I will admit, it was a bit traumatic having someone like that because it made me constantly hate myself and badly triggered me later when a guy I was dating after (that became my boyfriend later in life), said he is being held back from being with me because I don't have a flat stomach.

DEAR DIARY.......

That guy that became my boyfriend after that was so hesitant to be in an official relationship with me also became the boyfriend that I mentioned earlier that physically abused me. When he said he was hesitant to make things official because I don't have a flat stomach, I immediately felt sick to my stomach and got depressed. I still continued dating him (dumbass move I know) but found myself comparing my stomach to those that have a flat stomach and kept imaging myself that way. I kept thinking maybe I would be so much prettier if I just lost more weight. Mind you, my stomach wasn't that bad at all just a little muffin top. I cared so muchhhh about what my stomach looked liked that there would be times I ate little to no food each day.

DEAR DIARY.......

Every time I ate, I would feel ashamed of myself and imagine myself fatter as a result of eating. The food could have been healthy (which is what my usual diet consists of anyways) but I still would have felt fat no matter what. I hid it from him until Valentine's Day came around. Now Valentine's Day, I cooked him some seafood alfredo, lemon garlic butter potatoes, bought him chocolates, and wrote him a lovey dovey letter. Do you know what he got me? Absolutely NOTHING! I literally felt like an idiot doing so much for him and he didn't put any thought into making me feel special that day even though he knows how important Valentine's Day is to me. It is my favorite holiday since I love love, I love seeing others be loved, and brings me joy.

DEAR DIARY.......

I was holding back the whole entire day from crying the whole time I was with him. I was looking so forward to seeing him. I was so sad and quiet too. Later in the day, I finally stopped holding back my emotions and I let out all of my frustrations to him about how he doesn't make me feel loved, doesn't care about me, does the bare minimum, and how shallow he is for caring so fucking much about my stomach rather than my personality, the way I show love, the things I do for him, my romantic nature, the way I defend him, my efforts to make him happy, etc. I told him he should be ashamed of himself for that reason and I stormed off and started crying immediely afterwards. I cried the whole walk home. Everything I was holding in, I let out.

DEAR DIARY.......

We made up afterwards (yet another dumbass move lmao) and we stayed togther for a couple months. I broke up with him eventually because I felt like I was doing evrything in the relationship. I felt unloved and uncared for all the time. The only benefit I got from him was getting attention everyday.... but at what cost? You know what happened the next day? We got BACK together (lmao what is wrong with me). I really missed him and we talked and he said things will be better from now on. They were better for a bit, however, he was being super disrespectful to my friends. He would tell them to "move" when they sat next to me or would complain how they would "keep fucking talking". A completely different vibe from how he was before.

DEAR DIARY.......

After we got back together, it didn't last long maybe about two or three weeks. The day of the break up, we met up and I felt an uneasy vibe coming from him. We hanged out at his apartment's rooftop (the usual spot) and we were chilling and talking as usual. However, it didn't seem like he was interested or paying attention to anything I was saying. He just looked.... so angry. He eventually said out of the blue "suck my dick". I was puzzled and said "I was literally just talking why did you interrupt me and no". He said "a sexless relationship isn't going to fly with me so you're either going to fuck me or go home and fuck yourself". I choose to go home. I was tired of consistenly tolerating his rude ass behavior. It made him so fucking ugly.

DEAR DIARY.......

In his apartment, I need a key to use the elevators to get downstairs but I did not want to NEED him to get out the building so I used the staircase that leads to outside. It was about twelve floors or so that I had to walk down. When I got outside, there he was (surprise right). He started asking me why I was acting like that. We were arguing a bit but I don't think I was wrong because he was incredibly disrespectful. He then got angrier and grabbed my shirt back and forth ripping it and punched me a few times mainly in the back of my head. Him pulling on my shirt near my shoulder aggressively ended up bruising my left shoulder. My glasses fell when he started hitting me and I felt dizzy. He even stepped on my glasses and yelled "we are going to fuck NOW".

DEAR DIARY.......

I said no and he let go of me and he said "go home" which I was already doing in the first place hence why I took it upon myself to get downstairs by myself. I saw a police officer from across the street and immediately started walking towards him and told him that he hit me. He started saying "no I didn't she is fucking lying". Honestly, the police officer wasn't buying what he was saying I mean my shirt was ripped, my glasses were broke and bent, and my face was distraught. The officer started calling more police and my boyfriend (which then became my ex the moment he put his hands on me) started walking off. A man inside of a car got out and said he saw the whole thing and told me to please not go back with him.

DEAR DIARY.......

It took me awhile to fully process what just happened since my body was in such a state of shock and I started crying giving my full side of the story. I filed a report and my friend picked me up to drop me off home and bring me a new shirt. I wanted to hide all of this from my family. I did not want them to worry about me. I kept crying the whole time but I managed to clean my face up a bit before arriving home and faked a huge smile on my face and sounded like I had such a great night out with my friends. I then cried in the bathroom upstairs, went to bed, and cried myself to sleep. It was so traumatizing and the worst part was that most people I went to college with also knew him so I made a post about him to warm other women to protect them.

DEAR DIARY.......

I did this right before I fully went to sleep. I turned off my phone and went to sleep. When I woke up, I saw so many responses to the post I made. All of them were so supportive, loving, and caring. I was shocked people actually took the time to read and help me. It helped me feel better overall. People from college kept saying "I knew something was off about him". The crazy thing was that I always sensed something was off about him but I had no real reason to think something was off. I honesty just thought he was quiet and misunderstood. The moment he put his hands on me though, it all made sensed like the somewhat aggressive nature and the fact that one time he was arguing with his mom and she said "don't hit me".

DEAR DIARY……

Odd isn't it? Why would his mom say "don't hit me". Seems like a random thing to tell your son during an argument doesn't it? I am positive he has put his hands on her before. She may even be a little scared of him because he commands her all the time and is a little toooo comfortable being disrespectful towards her. She would just allow it and would never give him any consequences as a result. I was blind to it at first but I couldn't help but wonder afterwards if he ever hit her. I sweeped it under the rug and over a year later, he does that to me. Suddenly, everything became clear as day. One of my bestfriends at the time even asked a year before, "do you think he would ever hit you"? And I said "yeah, if he was mad enough"….

DEAR DIARY.......

The fact that I said that should've been a sign for me to leave way earlier but I had no exact proof that he was an abusive piece of shit, just a feeling and subtle signs. My intituion should've been enough. I need to trust it more rather than ending up self sabotaging myself like I always do. I think I self sabotage in hopes of changing the outcome that I KNOW will happen only for it to end EXACTLY how I predicted. I then end up in this toxic cycle where I'm heartbroken, crying all the time, feel lonely, question my self worth, feel worthless, asking what I did wrong, and sitting in my room alone at night bathing in my own self pity because I loved someone with my all and it still wasn't enough for them to love me with the same intensity.

DEAR DIARY.......

I think back to all the things I've done for them and makes me feel as though they're ungrateful. In reality, you just can't chase someone to love you or like you. You can't chase someone to adore you or appreciate you. I believe I have been chasing men to love me the same way I love them because for all of my life, I've just longed to feel special. I want to be the reason a guy looks forward to living life each day because he knows I will be a part of it. I want to be a great source of someone else's happiness. I want them excited to see me, genuinely care about me, and wants to make me happy. Love is something I have lacked all my life from family, friends, and significant others. I have gotten a lot of the opposite though unfortunately.

DEAR DIARY…….

Having family members say they hate me, certain family members spit on me, having my parents say nobody loves me except them, being molested growing up, being stalked, having to escape the possibility of getting rape by a family member everyday, having men I date compare my body or appearance to others, dating men that don't accept me for who I truly am, friends pretending to be my friend, friends backstabbing me, friends talking shit behind my back, my dad abandoning me for about two weeks right when I was born, my dad telling me to eat shit at the slightest arguments or disagreements, people I love forgetting my birthday, going through domestic abuse, and so much more has made me feel unloved.

DEAR DIARY.......

I haven't experienced much love in my life. I find myself dreaming and longing for love. I always ask myself, why is it so hard for me to obtain love? What am I doing wrong? What am I NOT doing when I try so hard to make everyone feel cared about? It is hard for me to open up to people since I honestly feel as though nobody cares about me and my problems. I have tried to open up in the past and for the most part have felt like they weren't paying attention, was waiting for me to shut up, blame me for what has happened to me, seem bored or fed up, or end up talking about themselves. Even when I am clearly in distress, I never really had that one person that will just check up on me to see how I am doing and if I am doing better.

DEAR DIARY.......

I mainly just have had people come into my life to cause me pain. The guy that molested me and tried to rape me everyday made my life a living hell everyday. I was constantly on the edge and feeling suicidal. He bullied me everyday for over a decade, kept stalking my moves, and would absolutely treat me like shit. He said he was in love with me, wants to be my first kiss, wants to be the one to take my virginity, would get overly jealous if he saw me interact with a guy, ruin my birthdays if i rejected his "needs", etc. I was NEVER interested in him and never will be because not only was he old as all hell..... he was a FAMILY MEMBER. He would try so hard to convince me that it is normal to have sex with someone you share blood with.

DEAR DIARY.......

I wanted so bad to just have a normal family relationship with him but he just didn't want to. Whenever I rejected him sexually, he would take it out on me or sometimes other family members. I would consistently lie and avoid him. I wanted to tell my family or the police but it was hard since he was family and we were poor so we relied on him heavily financially. I did not want my family to suffer as a result of his absence in his assistance to help provide for us. On my sweet sixteenth birthday, he wanted to have sex and i said no. Later that day, he threw a whole fit, kept yelling at me for no reason, was killing the happy vibes, dropped some cheese on the ground, blamed it on me, picked up the cheese, and rubbed it all over my face.

DEAR DIARY.......

Maybe it is just how I feel but I feel like as lonely and unloved I feel, I see happy and loved people everywhere I go even social media. For instance, on social media, I'll see birthday posts dedicated to someone they love, couples who appear clearly in love, baecations, loving comments on selfies, people saying they love someone publicly, etc. In person, it is similar except doesn't seem as perfect but still.... everyone seems happy and loved..... and then there is me. I realize maybe I try so hard to keep relationships with guys I date so that I can receive that type of treatment one day. I would love to be surprised by a romantic getaway, flowers, chocolates, a sweet social media post about me, and to be told that they love and appreciate me.

DEAR DIARY.......

I find myself disappointed on my birthday and Valentine's Day when I have someone because the energy I give to them on their birthday and Valentine's Day is no where as nearly reciprocated towards me. As I keep venting about my past love life, I realize maybe just maybe all of these men were placeholders in a way to fill in the lonely void. Maybe my acts of gift giving, love, care, words of affirmation, and acts of service come from a place of a fear of being lonely again rather than an act of passion. Most of the time after the break up, I find myself wondering what did I see in that person? I am telling myself they were't even all that for me to be crying over them or trying to heal over them. Sometimes during the relationship, I ask the same.

DEAR DIARY.......

There has been times where I would lose interest to a huge degree but still stay with them for whatever reason. Main reason has to be attachment since in a relationship, you talk to them and see them on a regular basis. When it's gone, there's this feeling of just emptiness almost like a piece of you is missing. After every break up no matter how bad it was, I always find myself wishing to recive a text from them rather it's a get back together text, an apology, or just casual texting. I find myself looking at my phone and getting excited from any notification I get hoping that it is them. I get disappointed and a bit sad when it's not them. Matter of fact, I hardly get notifications in general. Once we break up, my phone is dry as all hell.

DEAR DIARY.......

The only notifications I get are either weather warnings, phone battery status, Snapchat telling me someone posted a story, and the occasional messages from people I consider the closest to be my "friends" but even then it is always brief. I find myself to not feel so lonely when I post soemthing because it makes me feel like I am being seen and being payed attention to. I get actual notifications that actually pertain to me such as so and so "liked your photo", "liked yout story", "this user commented...", and so force. My posting can be a bit obsessive when I am trying to heal and feel lonely. I believe it is a way for me to escape my self destructive thoughts of being worthless, a burden, not worthy of love, and the occasional suicidal thoughts.

DEAR DIARY.......

Sometimes, dealing with my own emotions by myself in my room is the most dangerous place for me to be. I will remeber past trauma vividly, cry randomly, think about who would care if I died, think that my family's lives would be easier without me, replay hurtful words told to me, say harsh insults to myself, and play sad songs I relate to. When I go to sleep, it isn't always peaceful either. There has been plenty of times my dreams would replay traumatic events but in different ways or scenarios but always the same trauma. It is like a broken record. It is hard to escape the thoughts inside of my head. I am astonished I don't do any drugs or drink alcohol or take any anti depressant medication to escape my reality.

DEAR DIARY.......

I handle this thing we call life completely raw but I prefer it that way because it's real. I want to be in tuned with everything that is going on with and around me. I don't want to drown my sorrow in alcohol or put myself in a spiraling cycle of abusing drugs to prevent myself from dealing and feeling the emotions of everyday life. All the tribulations we experience in life are life's greatest teachers and build us to become wiser and become better. Had I not have gone through all these misfortunes in life, I would NOT be the person I am today. I would not change the person I am for anything in the world. I am not perfect but I know the people in my life feel loved, appreciated, and cared about by me. I've always wanted to be everyone's safe place..

DEAR DIARY.......

I know what it like to feel betrayed, uncared about, neglected, abandoned, heartbroken, suicidal, lonely, and etc. I know what it is like to try everything in my power to get rid of my depression only to be well for a short time only to go back to the same depressive state as before if not worse. There has been times that I would try to go out more, try new things, get out of my comfort zone, make new friends, and etc but only found myself faking my happiness most of the time and still feeling empty. Recently, I've been booking flights to different countries because life is too short to not travel but also to escape the feeling of existential loneliness. that I feel. I am going to these countries all by myself but maybe when I am there, I'll feel happy.

DEAR DIARY.......

I tell myself maybe if I am far away from all the people that have hurt me, abandoned me, betrayed me, shattered my heart, and caused my trauma that I will be in peace and it will take away all of those emotions I carry with me as if it never existed. Even if it doesn't change, I am willing to try. I rather be sad in Paris than my room. I am trying so hard to not be that person anymore by doing new things that scare me. Getting on a plane absolutely terrifies me but I am going to do it and I am going to like it. All I do is work, go to the gym, listen to rock and metal music, and go to sleep. I want to change my routine and grow as a person. I can't stay in this toxic cycle because if I don't change my routine, how can I expect my life and mental health to change.

DEAR DIARY.......

After some time has passed, I started practicing how I think mentally and what I tell myself. Although I have been heartbroken habitually, I tell myself I am worthy, I am beautiful inside and out, it's their loss not mines, my body is a temple, I am loved despite how lonely I feel everyday, I am smart, I am an amazing person, anyone would be lucky to be with me, and that just because someone did not love me in the same intensity that I loved them doesn't mean I am worthless or wasn't good enough. I learned the hard way that sometimes the way someone loves you is a projection of how they feel about themselves or sometimes things don't work out simply because you're not compatible with them and that is okay.

DEAR DIARY.......

How did I come to this conclusion? Well, remember that guy I mentioned earlier that kept ghosting me and was dating another girl at the same time as me? Well, he was barely ever there for himself. Yeah he would work consistently to get as much money as possible but overall he wasn't present for himself. He would say bad things things about himself, gain weight every time I saw him, did not care about the way he smelled or dressed, slept with almost one hundred women in his lifetime, had a temporary STD, etc. With that being said, how can I expect him to be present for me when he isn't even present with himself? With how you feel about yourself, you're either going to neglect them, love bomb. or love with balance.

DEAR DIARY.......

I have found myself unintentionally love bombing in relationships in the beginning because of the lack of presence or love I had for myself. The love I gave to others should've been the love that I should've gave to myself. In a relationship, I sorta lose myself and stop caring about my needs in order to completely cater to their needs. For example, I hated going to work so much because it was preventing me from seeing my boyfriend as much as I would like. However, I shouldn't have been that upset because I was literally making a lot of money which would benefit me more than working less just to see my boyfriend at the time. Additionally, for their birthdays, I would go all out while for mines I never really cared to do much for it.

DEAR DIARY.......

I would say I treated my boyfriends like kings while for myself I would do the bare minimum. I would feed myself, go to work, go to the gym, and sleep. I wasn't taking care of myself so much. My mental health needed work, I wasn't super motivated to elevate my life, did not care to work so much because I'd rather be with my man, and I did not care for my appearance after some time. I would just throw on whatever clothes I had and never switch up my hair or look. I need to work on myself at the same time while being with someone. But yeah I guess because I wasn't present for myself, it projected itself onto men I've dated by giving them all the love I had to give but to them instead. I guess I loved myself so little... I loved them so intensely.

DEAR DIARY.......

I find that when there is balance, that is the ideal. Two people in a relationship should both be working on themselves individually while being togther and loving one another. Looking back, I believe the men I've dated were overwhelmed by me doing so much for them all the time. Like imagine someone consistently saying sweet things to you, surprising you whenever they get the chance, getting showered by gifts, being showered by affection, etc. I will admit if I had a partner like that, I wouldn't know what to do. I wouldn't know how to repay them and what to do for them to show my appreciation. To be honest when it is consistent, I think the value of that partner overwhelming me with all those loving gestures would deteriorate.

DEAR DIARY.......

It wouldn't be special anymore. I would appreciate them yes but being overly spoiled would take away the excitement or value of their attempts to spoil me. Everything should be balanced. With that being said, I can see why men I've dated either lost feelings or started acting different towards me in a way that made me feel like they didn't love me and was taking me for granted. It makes sense why everything is so amazing in the beginning because I am not overwhelming them with anything yet. I'm just giving them my time and attention but not too much. You know tihinking back to all this, there was nothing really wrong with me. Do I love too much maybe too soon? Yes I do but it doesn't mean I am worthless or can't be loved.

DEAR DIARY.......

It means I need to take a step back, work on myself, and give my love to someone else in a balanced matter. I use to see couples all around me holding hands, sweet romantic posts on social media, romantic gift giving during Valentine's Day, and more and wonder when that will happen to me? I need to stop wondering and see that one day I will have that but I need to let that happen naturally. I learned this the hard way but you CANNOT chase someone to love you. You CANNOT buy their love and attention. You CANNOT do enormous things for someone and expect them to love you enormously. You CANNOT always have your schedule clear for them and expect them to also do the same for you.... it is not realistic.

DEAR DIARY.......

Back to compatibility, sometimes things don't work out simply because you guys aren't compatible. There may be nothing wrong with either of you guys but together as a unit, the two personalities may not blend well together and can do better with someone else. Does it mean you weren't good enough? Does it mean that the person they're with afterwards is better than you? Absolutely not. My abusive ex that I talked about earlier (before he became abusive) was a pretty decent boyfriend to me at the time during the begining. He texted me everyday and played virtual games with me all the time. I never felt alone when I was dating him. However, after some time, I realized him and I are just not compatible and it made me feel bad at the time.

DEAR DIARY……

It made me feel bad because in my mind, he hasn't done anything wrong. I couldn't wrap my head around why I would lose interest for someone that is giving me so much attention. We had little to no chemistry. There was times where we would have fun and engaging conversations but it was always rare. It was much easier to have those type of conversations with him via text messages but in person it was so much harder for him to be able to hold a conversation. I found that he was super dismissive when it came to any conversation that was remotely considered sad, serious, or deep. I am a very sensitive, emphatic, sympathetic, and emotional person. Deep conversations are an absolute MUST for me.

DEAR DIARY.......

If I can't have deep conversations with someone, it will NEVER work out. I always feel a much deeper connection with someone after I have poured my inner deepest thoughts to someone and vice versa. Deep conversations make me feel heard and stimulate my mind. I find myself in a much better mood every time. With him, it was like he only wanted to have goofy and upbeat conversations and that to me isn't realistic. Life is filled with tribulations, plot twists, fond memories, funny moments, love, lessons, loss, ups, downs, and so much more. Just talking about life in a one dimensional way is not realistic. We must talk about all aspects of life not just the good part because who DOESN'T go through things in life?

DEAR DIARY.......

Remember that guy I briefly mentioned that cheated on me? Well we dated for five months and I must say it was the most boring relationship of my life and also the first relationship I've had. I was still learning about what I liked and to be honest I settled because I thought I couldn't find anything else since I was so insecure back then. Anyways, we had no chemistry whatsoever. The relationship only lasted five months because I was attached to him. I was attached to the daily attention he was giving me but in truth, we weren't compatible at all. We never really had stuff to talk about and barely ever had fun with one another. He would also ignore me a lot. He actually had much better chemistry with the girl he cheated on me with.

DEAR DIARY.......

I saw how well they both held a conversation with one another and it made me feel jealous at the time. They were laughing a lot with one another and via text they both opened up to each other by trauma sharing while with me he just kept it goofy and would often leave me feeling abandoned by playing video games instead of spending time with me. I foreshadowed he would cheat, it was only a matter of time. Lord and behold a few weeks later, the girl he cheated on me with told me that they made out for about five minutes. Mind you, she was also my "friend". I wasn't surprised but I was hurt. I messaged him and asked him if it was true. He left me on read for a day then replied saying it was true and that he was so sorry.

DEAR DIARY.......

Honestly, the relationship died a long time ago like a month in and I knew it wasn't going to last. I actually had better chemistry and bonds with other people, I just wasn't into them romantically. I was wondering what I did wrong and blamed myself for him cheating on me. After some healing, I realized it just wasn't meant to be because we didn't have good chemistry and the only thing that made us stay together for as long as we did was the attachment. There wasn't anything actually wrong with me since I was a very good girlfriend to him but you can only make a relationship work if you're compatible with them. The lack of compatability doesn't make me any less of a person or any less good of a girlfriend. I was just with the wrong person.

DEAR DIARY.......

After much reflection, despite all the shit I talked about the guys I dated earlier, I can say they all gave me some pretty good memories and made me feel loved and cared for at one point. My cheating ex boyfriend made me feel like I could actually get men so he was my introduction to the world of dating. The guy I dated for four years on and off has made me feel loved and cared about a lot despite his toxic behavior at times. He always got me something thoughtful for Valentines Day, told me he loves me, would write sweet paragraphs to me, made sure I wasn't mad at him for long, pay for me at times, be super affectionate towards me, we would have sleepovers, a lot of deep conversations, etc.

DEAR DIARY.......

There was this guy I dated for only about two months or so and although our time together was short romantically, he was a good boyfriend. He made me feel heard everyday, would be there for me, would call and text me everyday, always compliment my pictures on social media, and we had good chemistry. Our time togther was short and actucally not toxic at all but it taught me that break ups can still happen even if there is nothing wrong with either person in the relationship... sometimes things just happen out of one's control. There was this other guy I dated on and off for about a year or so. Things ended because he was a pathological liar, kept gaslighting me, ungrateful, fake, and too flirtatious to any girl.

DEAR DIARY.......

Despite all of that being said, he did give me some good memories especially in the beginning but also throughout. Every time I was sad, he could tell and would always try to get out of me what was wrong. He would drive me around a lot, pay for my food a couple times, would be a good shoulder to cry on, easy to be vulnerable with especially since he was always vulnerable towards me, would do things with me when I would be sad so that I can feel better, and would give good advice to me. My abusive ex use to always try to spend time with me, play virtual games with me, tell me he loves me, have my back towards his misogynistic mother all the time, talk to me everyday somehow someway, go anywhere I wanted, listen to my music taste, etc.

DEAR DIARY……

He was very open minded to all of my interests. It was like he wanted to know everything about me about what made me…. me. That made me feel very special and meant a lot to me since I never really had someone truly try to get to know all of my interests especially music since I only listen to metal and rock music. The guy I mentioned a few times that kept ghosting me also gave me fond memories despite his deceitful behavior and inconsistency. He has been a listening ear to a lot such as family problems, confusion with life, problems with guys I've dated, etc. It was fairly easy to open up to him and he would always try to give advice as best as he could and would always say he would always be there for me.

DEAR DIARY.......

He has driven me home everytime, bought me a drink once, gave me my first cigar experience (even though I didn't like it nor asked for it), has offered me to move in with him sometime whenever he gets a place to escape my toxic family situation, gave good business advice to me since I am a business owner, gave me a hug when he found out nobody really came to my birthday party except him and another friend, and all around a good friend. Very inconsistent but a good friend nonetheless. He wasn't a very good partner but there has been times he made me feel loved. He was a much better friend more than anything. He gave me some sort of closure instead of letting me just suffer in my thoughts when everything was over.

DEAR DIARY…….

He also helped encouraged me to travel. I always wanted to travel but always prevented myself from doing so because I grew up as a sheltered child. I was overly protected too much my whole life which prevented me from experiencing the real world and forming some sort of independence. It wasn't until two years ago out of my twenty six years of life that I finally truly formed a good amount of it. Money was the main issue. My father's way of controlling me growing up was threatening me by trying to take away money which we needed if I didn't do as he said. He would say things like "I won't pay the rent or buy the groceries if you don't…." which looking back was super manipulative, toxic, and just plain shitty.

DEAR DIARY.......

It made me feel like I couldn't do anything in life almost like I was living for my dad. He did the same with my mom as well. He took advantage of the fact that me, my mom, and brother didn't work. Once I started working, that is when my independence finally started and my fear of him finally going away little by little. I am still to this day still becoming more independent. It is a process and it isn't an easy one that solves itself overnight. It has taken me a lot of logical thinking, hard work, prayers, strength, a positive mindset, tears, sweat, and more but every year and day it gets easier. I know one day I will have everything I want and deserve out of this life. I believe good things happen to good people and an abundance of my life has proven that.

DEAR DIARY.......

I was going to travel regardless but it probably would've taken longer if I didn't have those talks with that guy about my family issues all the time. He really listened to me, gave his insight, and tried to come up with solutions. He gave me that extra push to do so and I appreciate that because now I am finally doing all the things that scare me but also excite me at the same time. I have multiple trips in store for me. I am constantly learning new things about myself after all the heartbreaks, manipulation, mistakes, accomplishments, and trauma I have experienced. I may feel alone and unloved all the time but it doesn't mean I am. Working on myself, loving me, and learning new things without boundaries is how I will live my life.

DEAR DIARY.......

I am convinced that when you are a good person, good things come back to you. Whatever comes around goes around. Bad things happen to everyone but the universe will always reward good people. I may have gone through hell and back but things eventually got better. When the Covid-19 pandemic happened, my life started improving. My dad use to come every single day to cause annoyance and toxicity everyday but once the pandemic happened, he visited so much less often and it stayed that way even now. It was a breath of fresh air. I love my dad but not seeing him everyday was one of the best things that ever happened to me. My mental health and sanity had drastically improved since then.

DEAR DIARY.......

I had to literally escape rape everyday of my life growing up and even for a good portion of my adult life but guess what? I didn't get raped at the end of the day and I am forever grateful that my innocence wasn't stolen by a horny family member for his own selfish gain. I could've called the police as I had records of text messages of him stating his intentions but unfortunately, he was a huge assistance to my family financially and I didn't want my family to suffer as a result so I choose to be the only one to suffer instead. I cared about my abuser a lot and the thought of him in jail broke my heart. I just wanted to find another solution but overtime, he gave up which I will be always be grateful for because I really didn't deserve that.

DEAR DIARY.......

I am also thankful for all of my break ups and heartbreaks because it has built my wisdom and made me love myself more. I upgrade every time I get heartbroken. My life improves so much after, I look better, and the man I get afterwards is always better than the last. When the break up is fresh, I am devastated and can't imagine my life without them but later on, I want to continue to not have them in my life because life gets so much better without them. It is one of the best feelings when you stop giving a fuck about them romantically. My exes have tried to come back but I have declined. I elevate and the experience of me falling in love again with someone else is always so much greater than the last person I was in love with.

DEAR DIARY.......

Every bad person that has done me wrong has experienced karma in some shape or form. That guy that kept ghosting me has gone through a lot of car accidents, broke his finger, broke his toe, bruised his ribs, had his stomach pumped, has had covid multiple times, got hit by a car, had a concussion, etc during the time he was dating me and deceiving me. My abusive ex remains to not have any friends except his mom and a boring life. All of my other exes just have no access to me or are suffering in their present relationships. My toxic family members are suffering in their love life and struggling financially. They never experienced true genuine love and they never really get to keep most of their money that they make.

DEAR DIARY.......

I on the other hand, have multiple trips to look forward to, my own businesses, a fun job where I love all of my co-workers, built better bonds with people, experienced endless concerts of bands I adore, have had multiple amazing nights out, have had things turn out in my favor unexpectedly most of the time, etc. It is like God doesn't want me to be sad especially for long. I am not saying I am happy that karma has gotten to them but it does goes to show that what you put into this world is what you get back. I truly believe that because I am a good person who thinks positive, has helped people, given life advice to people that needed it, loved people with my all, do things with good intentions, etc that my life has manifested itself into a good one now.

SOME TIME LATER........

DEAR DIARY.......

I am completely healed. I don't let my traumas define me, I am not fixated on the past, I love myself so much more, and I am finally happy. I am having the time of my life traveling to different places, I faced my fear of getting on a plane and I LOVE it, and I finally experienced a true gentleman. I never thought a guy would ever take me out on a date and pay almost two hundred dollars, insist I get more food or drinks, shows he cares in a way that I KNOW he cares about me rather than question, give me his jacket when it is cold outside to make sure I am warm, and just effortlessly be so sweet towards me. No matter where this goes, I know I am capable of being loved and I am optismisitc for the future of my quality of life and future love life.

Love yourself fiercely before you love someone else, give yourself daily positive affirmations, laugh, cry, and take in life's greatest teachers. You only live once so make a life that you that you will be proud of.

—Yasmin Isabel Velasquez.

Made in the USA
Middletown, DE
03 December 2022

16030242R10046